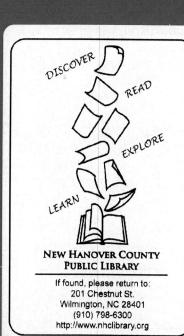

Teach Me...™
Everyday
ITALIAN
Volume 1

Written by Judy Mahoney
Illustrated by Patrick Girouard

Technology is changing our world. Far away exotic places have literally become neighbors. We belong to a global community and our children are becoming "global kids." Comparing and understanding different languages and cultures is more vital than ever! Additionally, learning a foreign language reinforces a child's overall education. Early childhood is the optimal time for children to learn a second language, and the Teach Me Everyday Language Series is a practical and inspiring way to teach them. Through story and song, each book and audio encourages them to listen, speak, read and write in a foreign language.

Today's "global kids" hold tomorrow's world in their hands. So when it comes to learning a new language, don't be surprised when they say, "teach me!"

Italian is a Romance language and the official language of Italy. Each region of Italy has its own dialect, though the Tuscan dialect is the main language of literature and media. The Italian alphabet omits using the English letters J, K, W, X and Y except for non-native words. Many Italian words are similar to the English equivalent and are already part of the everyday vocabulary like pizza, ravioli and bambino. And notice that most Italian words end in a vowel!

Teach Me Everyday Italian
Volume One
ISBN 13: 978-1-59972-107-1
Library of Congress PCN: 2008902659

Copyright © 2008 by Teach Me Tapes, Inc.
6016 Blue Circle Drive, Minnetonka, MN 55343
www.teachmetapes.com

Book Design by Design Lab, Northfield, MN

10 9 8 7 6 5 4 3 2

INDEX & SONG LIST

Più noi siamo insieme ♪ ♫

Più noi siamo sieme, insieme, insieme
Più noi siamo sieme, più felici noi siam
I tuoi amici sono i miei
I miei amici sono i tuoi
Più noi siamo insieme, più felici noi siam.

The More We Get Together

The more we get together, together, together
The more we get together, the happier we'll be
For your friends are my friends
And my friends are your friends
The more we get together, the happier we'll be.

Il mio gatto.
Lui si chiama Fufi.
È grigio.

My cat.
His name is Fuffi.
He is gray.

il mio gatto

Il mio cane.
Lui si chiama Medoro.
È bianco e nero.

il mio cane

My dog.
His name is Medoro.
He is white and black.

Ed ecco la mia casa. Ha un tetto marrone e un giardino con dei fiori gialli.

Here is my house. It has a brown roof and a garden with yellow flowers.

La mia camera è celeste.
Sono le sette.
Svegliati!
Svegliati!

My room is blue.
It is seven o'clock.
Wake up!
Wake up!

L'allodola
**Allodola, gentile allodola
Allodola, io ti spennerò
Io ti spennerò il becco
Io ti spennerò il becco
E il becco, e il becco.**

The Lark
Lark, oh lovely lark
Lark, I will pluck you now
I will pluck your little beak
I will pluck your little beak
And your beak, and your beak.

Fra' Martino
**Fra' Martino, campanaro
Dormi tu? Dormi tu?
Suona le campane
Suona le campane
Din don dan!
Din don dan!**

Are You Sleeping
Are you sleeping, are you sleeping
Brother John? Brother John?
Morning bells are ringing
Morning bells are ringing
Ding dang dong!
Ding dang dong!

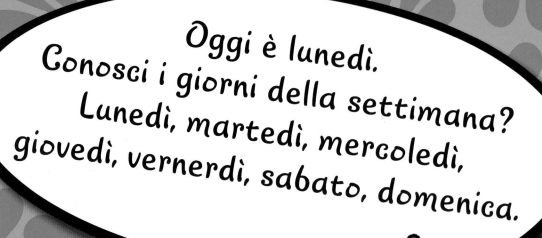

Today is Monday.
Do you know the days of the week?
Monday, Tuesday, Wednesday,
Thursday, Friday, Saturday, Sunday.

LUNEDÌ Monday

MARTEDÌ Tuesday

MERCOLEDÌ Wednesday

GIOVEDÌ Thursday

VERNERDÌ Friday

SABATO Saturday

DOMENICA Sunday

I get dressed.
I put on my shirt,
my pants, my shoes
and my hat.

Testa, spalle, ginocchia e piedi ♪

Testa, spalle, ginocchia e piedi, ginocchia e piedi
Testa, spalle, ginocchia e piedi, ginocchia e piedi
Ho due occhi, un naso, una bocca e due orecchie
Testa, spalle, ginocchia e piedi, ginocchia e piedi.

Head, Shoulders, Knees and Toes
Head and shoulders, knees and toes, knees and toes
Head and shoulders, knees and toes, knees and toes
Eyes and ears and mouth and nose
Head and shoulders, knees and toes, knees and toes.

Faccio colazione.
Mi piace il pane, il burro e la marmellata e bevo il latte.

I eat breakfast. I like bread with butter and jam, and drink milk.

The weather is bad. It is raining.
I cannot go for a walk today.

Rain Medley

Rain, rain, go away
Come again another day
Rain, rain, go away
Little Johnny wants to play.

It's raining, it's pouring
The old man is snoring
He bumped his head and went to bed
And couldn't get up in the morning.

Pioggia, vattene via

Pioggia, vattene via
Torna un altro giorno
Gianni vuol giocare
Pioggia, vattene via.

L'arcobaleno

A volte blu e a volte verde
I colori più belli che ho mai visto
Rosa e viola, giallo - sì!
Amo cavalcar quest' arcobalen.

Rainbows

Sometimes blue and sometimes green
Prettiest colors I've ever seen
Pink and purple, yellow - whee!
I love to ride those rainbows.

Ecco la mia scuola.
Dico, "Buongiorno, Signora Maestra."
Ripeto i numeri e l'alfabeto.

SCHOOL

la mia scuola

Here is my school.
I say, "Good morning, teacher."
I repeat my numbers and my alphabet.

i numeri

1 uno 2 due 3 tre 4 quattro 5 cinque 6 sei 7 sette 8 otto 9 nove 10 dieci

Numbers
one   two   three   four   five   six   seven   eight   nine   ten

l'alfabeto

A a (ah)   B b (bi)   C c (ci)   D d (di)

E e (ee)   F f (effe)   G g (gi)   H h (acca)   I i (i)   L l (elle)

M m (emme)   N n (enne)   O o (o)   P p (pi)   Q q (cu)

R r (erre)   S s (esse)   T t (ti)   U u (u)   V v (vi/vu)   Z z (zeta)

Ed e' tutto qui. Ora sogno A B C. Canta insieme e vieni qui.

i (lunga)   k (kappa)   w (vi/vu doppia)   v (ics)   y (i greca)

Alphabet

A	B	C	D	E	F	G
H	I	L	M	N	O	P
Q	R	S	T	U	V	Z

Now I know my ABC's, next time won't you sing with me?

i   k   w   v   y

(Note: these 5 letters only used in words without Italian origin)

Maria aveva un agnellino 🎵🎵

Maria aveva un agnellin, un agnellin, un agnellin
Maria aveva un agnellin, di lana bianca e pura
Ovunque Maria andava, andava, andava
Ovunque Maria andava, l'agnello la seguiva.

Mary Had a Little Lamb
Mary had a little lamb, little lamb, little lamb
Mary had a little lamb, its fleece was white as snow
Everywhere that Mary went, Mary went, Mary went
Everywhere that Mary went, the lamb was sure to go.

Un elefante
Due elefanti andaron a giocar
Molto vicino a un alvear
Si divertivan talmente insiem
Che si chiamavan l'un l'altro, vien!

Tre elefanti...
Quattro elfanti...
Tutti gli elefanti...

One Elephant
One elephant went out to play
Upon a spiders web one day
He had such enormous fun
That he called for another elephant to come.

Two elephants...
Three elephants...
Four elephants...
All the elephants...

*Traditional English version uses "spider's web", Italian uses "bee hive".

Così fan

Così fan, fan, fan
Le graziose marionette
Così fan, fan, fan
Tre giretti e poi sen van.

Ma poi torneran
Le graziose marionette
Ma poi torneran
E i ragazzi cresceran.

The Marionettes

So they do, do, do
The pretty marionettes
So they do, do, do
Three turns and they're through.

But they will come back
Our pretty marionettes
But they will come back
And the children will grow up.

Dopo la scuola, andiamo a casa in macchina.

After school,
we go home by car.

Le ruote della macchina

Le ruote della macchina girano e girano
Girano e girano, girano e girano
Le ruote della macchina girano e girano
Per tutta la città.

Il clacson dell' auto fa tut tut tut
Tut tut tut, tut tut tut
Il clacson dell' auto fa tut tut tut
Per tutta la città.

I bimbi nella macchina "andiamo a mangiare"
"Abbiamo fame, abbiamo fame"
I bimbi nella macchina "andiamo a mangiare"
Per tutta la città.

The Wheels on the Car
The wheels on the car go round and round
Round and round, round and round
The wheels on the car go round and round
All around the town.

The horn on the car goes beep beep beep
Beep beep beep, beep beep beep
The horn on the car goes beep beep beep
All around the town.

The children in the car go, "Let's have lunch"
"Let's have lunch, let's have lunch"
The children in the car go, "Let's have lunch"
All around the town.

Dormi bel bambino

Dormi bel bambino dormi in silenzio
Papà ti comprerà un bel canarino
Se il canarino non canterà
Un anello di diamanti ti comprerà
Se i diamanti non brilleranno
Papà ti comprerà uno specchio dorato
Se poi lo specchio si romperà
Sempre sarai la gioia di papà.

Hush Little Baby
Hush little baby don't say a word
Papa's going to buy you a mockingbird
If that mockingbird won't sing
Papa's going to buy you a diamond ring
If that diamond ring turns brass
Papa's going to buy you a looking glass
If that looking glass falls down
You'll still be the sweetest little baby in town.

Dopo il pisolino, andiamo al parco. Vedo delle papere. Canto, danzo sul ponte con i miei amici.

After our naps, we go to the park. I see the ducks. I sing, I dance on the bridge with my friends.

Sopra il ponte d'Avignone

Sopra il ponte d'Avignone
Noi danziamo, noi danziamo
Sopra il ponte d'Avignone
Noi danziamo con passione.

On the Bridge of Avignon

On the bridge of Avignon
They're all dancing, they're all dancing
On the bridge of Avignon
They're all dancing round and round.

Giro giro tondo

Giro giro tondo
Il mare è fondo
Tonda è la Terra
Tutti giù per terra.

Giro giro tondo
Casca il mondo
Casca la Terra
Tutti giù per terra.

Traditional Song

Turn around and around
Deep is the ocean
The earth is round
All down to the ground.

Turn around and around
The world falls down
So falls the earth
All down to the ground.

Sei papere

Sei papere che io conoscevo
Grandi, piccole, o tanto carine
Ma una papera con la piuma sul dorso
Guidava le altre col suo
Qua qua qua
Qua qua qua
Qua qua qua
Guidava le altre col suo
Qua qua qua.

Six Little Ducks

Six little ducks that I once knew
Fat ones, skinny ones, fair ones, too
But the one little duck with the feather on his back
He led the others with his
Quack quack quack
Quack quack quack
Quack quack quack
He led the others with his
Quack quack quack.

C'è un topolino

C'è un topolino, nel granaio
Sento il gatto miagolare
C'è un topolino, nel granaio
Sento il gatto miagolare
Io sento, io sento, sento il gatto, miao miao
Io sento, io sento, sento il gatto, miagolar.

There's a Mouse

There's a mouse, in the barn
I hear the cat meowing
There's a mouse, in the barn
I hear the cat meowing
I hear, I hear, I hear the cat, meow meow
I hear, I hear, I hear the cat, meowing.

Uhm! Ho fame.
È l'ora di cena.

I am hungry.
It is dinner time.

Oh! Susanna

Vengo or dall' Alabama, con il banjo mio fedel
E mi reco in Luisiana, per trovare il mio amor
Oh! Susanna, non piangere per me
Vengo or dall' Alabama, con il banjo mio fedel.

Oh! Susanna
Well, I come from Alabama with my banjo on my knee
Goin' to Louisiana, my true love for to see
Oh, Susanna, won't you cry for me
'Cause I come from Alabama with my banjo on my knee.

È notte.
Vedi le stelle in cielo?

It is night time.
Do you see the stars
in the sky?

Lucciola, lucciola

Lucciola, lucciola, vien da me
Ti darò il pan del re
Il pan del re e della regina
Lucciola, lucciola, vien vicina
Lucciola, lucciola, vien da me
Ti darò il pan del re.

Firefly, Firefly

Firefly, firefly, come to me
I will give you the king's bread
The king's bread and the queen's
Firefly, firefly, come to close to me
Firefly, firefly, come to me
I will give you the king's bread.

Ninna nanna

Buona notte, o gentil
Chiudi gli occhi al riposo
Tra ghirlande di fior
Dal profumo sottil.

Una dolce canzon
Possa i sogni cullare
E ti possa destar
Quando l'alba verrà.

Italian Lullaby

Good night, sweet baby
Close your eyes and rest
Among garlands of flowers
With their gentle perfume.

A lovely song
May sooth your dreams
And you wake up
When dawn will come.

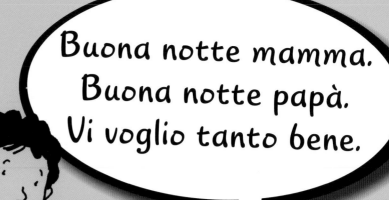

Buona notte mamma.
Buona notte papà.
Vi voglio tanto bene.

Goodnight Mommy.
Goodnight Daddy.
I love you.

Buona notte cari amici

Buona notte, cari amici, buona notte
Buona notte, cari amici, buona notte
Buona notte
Buona notte
Buona notte, cari amici, buona notte.

Buona notte! Arriverderci! Ciao!

Goodnight My Friends
Goodnight, my friends, goodnight
Goodnight, my friends, goodnight
Goodnight, my friends
Goodnight, my friends
Goodnight, my friends, goodnight.
Goodnight! Goodbye! See you!

Vuoi saperne di più?
(Want to learn more?)

lampada

banjo

divano

palla

cane

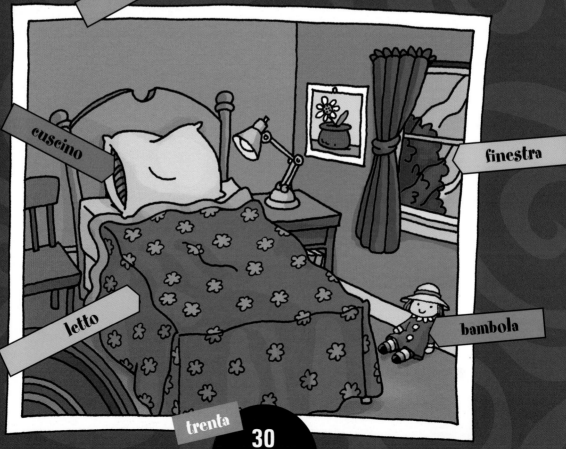

cuscino

finestra

letto

bambola

cioccolato caldo

succo d'arancia

pane

marmellata

albero

amico

ponte

pallone da calcio

colori

rosso

viola

blu

verde

arancione

grigio

giallo

rosa

marrone

bianco

nero